T0023919

ORCHIDS

Orchids

Orchids

Humans have long been fascinated by orchids – a large plant family with thousands of species found all around the world, producing flowers in myriad shapes and colours.
They were symbols of virility for the ancient Greeks, and have also come to represent everything from strength and luxury to love and beauty.

From rare and delicate species hiding deep in remote rainforests, to the large and gaudy blooms that adorn many peoples'

homes today, orchids have captured our imaginations the world over, and inspired many a writer, poet and artist.

This beautiful book combines gorgeous watercolour paintings and other artworks of orchids with quotes about nature and life in general, from the deep and meaningful to the light hearted and frivolous.

"*Look deep into nature,
and then you will understand
everything better.*"

– ALBERT EINSTEIN

"*Mama was my greatest teacher, a teacher of compassion, love and fearlessness. If love is sweet as a flower, then my mother is that sweet flower of love.*"

– STEVIE WONDER

"*If you're quiet, you're not living. You've got to be noisy and colourful and lively.*"

– MEL BROOKS

*"Life is a long lesson
in humility."*

– JAMES M. BARRIE

"The marsh, to him who enters it in a receptive mood, holds, besides mosquitoes and stagnation, melody, the mystery of unknown waters, and the sweetness of Nature undisturbed by man."

– WILLIAM BEEBE

"Find beauty not only in the thing itself but in the pattern of the shadows, the light and dark which that thing provides."

– JUNICHIRO TANIZAKI

"I love slippers, but I have five dogs. So unfortunately, I have a lot of single slippers."

– GEORGINA BLOOMBERG

"*Pull the string, and it will follow wherever you wish. Push it, and it will go nowhere at all.*"

– DWIGHT D. EISENHOWER

"If we lose bees, we may be looking at losing apples and oranges. We may be looking at losing a great deal of other crops as well, and other animals that depend on those crops."

– ANNALEE NEWITZ

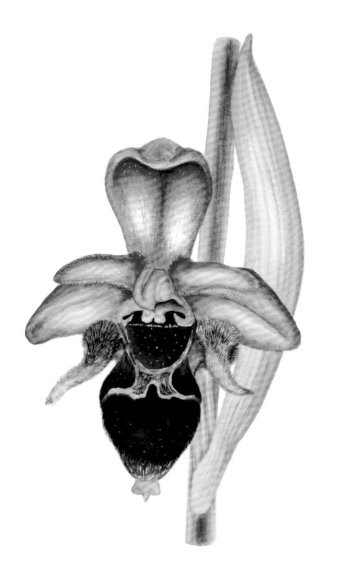

"To describe the overwhelming life of a tropical forest just in terms of inert biochemistry and DNA didn't seem to give a very full picture of the world."

– RUPERT SHELDRAKE

"*Watercolour is a swim in the metaphysics of life... a mirror of one's own character. Let it be unpredictable and colourful.*"

– ANONYMOUS

"*Keep your face to the sun and you will never see the shadows.*"

– HELEN KELLER

"*I decided that if I could paint that flower in a huge scale, you could not ignore its beauty.*"

– GEORGIA O'KEEFFE

"*Inspiration arrives as a packet of material to be delivered.*"

– JOHN UPDIKE

" 'Welcome to the family,
Zane,' she said, and the
sincerity in her voice
made his throat tighten.
'I wish I'd known earlier,
but if wishes was dollars,
I'd be the Queen of Sheba.' "

– ABIGAIL ROUX

"The job of the artist is always to deepen the mystery."

– FRANCIS BACON

"*People always like things that seem exotic.*"

– JANE BIRKIN

"When the flower blooms,
the bees come uninvited."

– RAMAKRISHNA

"An orchid in a deep forest
sends out its fragrance
even if no one is around to
appreciate it."

– CONFUCIUS

"*Beauty is eternity gazing at itself in a mirror.*"

– KHALIL GIBRAN

"Do not waste time dreaming of great faraway opportunities; do the best you can where you are. Open your petals of power and beauty and fling out the fragrance of your life in the place that has been assigned to you."

– ORISON SWETT MARDEN

"A writer without a pen would be like a duck without water!"

– DONOVAN

"Sadly, it's much easier to create a desert than a forest."

– JAMES LOVELOCK

"Lord Illingworth told me this morning that there was an orchid there as beautiful as the seven deadly sins."

– OSCAR WILDE

"Don't cry because it's over.
Smile because it happened."

– DR SEUSS

"Hope is being able to see
that there is light despite
all of the darkness."

– DESMOND TUTU

"*The essence of the beautiful is unity in variety.* "

– FELIX MENDELSSOHN

"*Life is the flower for which love is the honey.*"

– VICTOR HUGO

"Climb the mountains and get their good tidings. Nature's peace will flow into you as sunshine flows into trees."

– JOHN MUIR

"My books were always full of ink blots, always stained and covered with smeared sketches and pictures, which one draws idly when his attention wanders from his task."

– PIERRE LOTI

"To rise above the treeline is to go above thought, and after, the descent back into bird song, bog orchids, willows and firs is to sink into the preliterate parts of ourselves."

– GRETEL EHRLICH

"Blessed are they who see beautiful things in humble places where other people see nothing."

– CAMILLE PISSARRO

"*Travel is a state of mind. It has nothing to do with existence or the exotic. It is almost always an inner experience.*"

– PAUL THEROUX

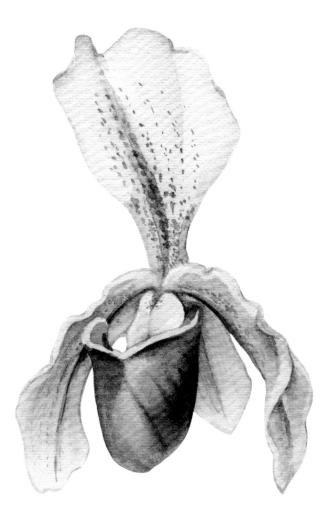

"Art, in itself,
is an attempt to bring
order out of chaos."

– STEPHEN SONDHEIM

"A flower is not better when it blooms than when it is merely a bud; at each stage it is the same thing – a flower in the process of expressing its potential."

– PAULO COELHO

"Beauty is a short-lived tyranny."

– SOCRATES

"*Destroying rainforest for economic gain is like burning a Renaissance painting to cook a meal.*"

– E. O. WILSON

"When two friends
understand each other totally,
the words are soft and strong
like an orchid's perfume."

– SARA JEANNETTE DUNCAN

"*For my part I know nothing with any certainty, but the sight of the stars makes me dream.*"

– VINCENT VAN GOGH

"*Happiness is a butterfly, which when pursued, is always just beyond your grasp, but which, if you will sit down quietly, may alight upon you.*"

– NATHANIEL HAWTHORNE

"*It is a mistake to look too far ahead. Only one link of the chain of destiny can be handled at a time.*"

– WINSTON CHURCHILL

"*If your heart is a volcano, how shall you expect flowers to bloom?*"

– KHALIL GIBRAN

"*If nature were not beautiful, it would not be worth knowing, and if nature were not worth knowing, life would not be worth living.*"

– HENRI POINCARE

"*The purpose of art is washing the dust of daily life off our souls.*"

– PABLO PICASSO

"Nobody climbs mountains for scientific reasons. Science is used to raise money for the expeditions, but you really climb for the hell of it."

– EDMUND HILLARY

"Sunrise paints the sky
with pinks and the sunset
with peaches. Cool to warm.
So is the progression from
childhood to old age."

– VERA NAZARIAN

"*I also like to garden.
I grow things, vegetables,
flowers. I particularly
like orchids. I raise orchids.*"

– BEAU BRIDGES

"I never saw a wild thing sorry for itself. A small bird will drop frozen dead from a bough without ever having felt sorry for itself."

– D. H. LAWRENCE

"How many thorns of human nature are bristling conceits, buds of promise grown sharp for want of congenial climate."

– JOHN BURROUGHS

"For other people, love is like some rare orchid that can only grow in one place under a certain set of conditions. For me it's like bindweed. It grows with no encouragement at all, under any conditions, and just strangles everything else."

– SCARLETT THOMAS

"*By plucking her petals,
you do not gather the
beauty of the flower.*"

– RABINDRANATH TAGORE

"My dream is to one day afford a real pair of ruby slippers. For me, they will always be the ultimate shoe."

– CAMILLA LUDDINGTON

"A thing of beauty
is a joy forever:
its loveliness increases;
it will never pass
into nothingness."

– JOHN KEATS

"I did not want to be a tree, a flower or a wave. In a dancer's body, we as audience must see ourselves, not the imitated behaviour of everyday actions, not the phenomenon of nature, not exotic creatures from another planet, but something of the miracle that is a human being."

– MARTHA GRAHAM

"*Beauty is truth's smile when she beholds her own face in a perfect mirror.*"

– RABINDRANATH TAGORE

"I am an old man and have known a great many troubles, but most of them never happened."

– MARK TWAIN

"I was a punk before it got its name. I had that hairstyle and purple lipstick."

– VIVIENNE WESTWOOD

*"The bird a nest,
the spider a web,
man friendship."*

– WILLIAM BLAKE

"*Despite everything,
I believe that people
are really good at heart.*"

– ANNE FRANK

"*The flame of anger,
bright and brief,
sharpens the barb of love.*"

– WALTER SAVAGE LANDOR

"The orchid is Mother Nature's masterpiece."

– ROBYN

Published in 2023 by Reed New Holland Publishers
Sydney

Level 1, 178 Fox Valley Road, Wahroonga, NSW 2076, Australia

newhollandpublishers.com

Copyright © 2023 Reed New Holland Publishers

All rights reserved. No part of this publication may be reproduced, stored in a retrieval system or transmitted, in any form or by any means, electronic, mechanical, photocopying, recording or otherwise, without the prior written permission of the publishers and copyright holders.

A record of this book is held at the National Library of Australia.

ISBN 978 1 92107 367 0

Managing Director: Fiona Schultz
Publisher and Project Editor: Simon Papps
Designer: Andrew Davies
Production Director: Arlene Gippert
Printed in China

10 9 8 7 6 5 4 3 2 1

OTHER TITLES BY REED NEW HOLLAND INCLUDE:

A Complete Guide to Native Orchids of Australia (Third Edition)
David L. Jones
ISBN 978 1 92554 671 2

Native Plants of Northern Australia (New Edition)
John Brock
ISBN 978 1 87706 924 6

A Photographic Guide to Wildflowers of Outback Australia
Denise Greig
ISBN 978 1 86436 805 5

Australian Native Plants
John W. Wrigley and Murray Fagg
ISBN 978 1 87706 940 6

Field Guide to Australian Wildflowers
Denise Greig
ISBN 978 1 86436 334 0

Reed Concise Guide: Wildflowers of Australia
Ken Stepnell
ISBN 978 1 92151 755 6

For details of these books and hundreds of other Natural History titles see newhollandpublishers.com and follow ReedNewHolland on Facebook

f